KEY

- Species marked ~~with this icon~~ ● ~~are~~ pollinators.
- Species marked with this icon **P** are pests.
- Species marked with these icons **V** or **B** are either an aesthetic garden visitor or a beneficial predator of pest species.
- Species marked with this icon **D** spread plant disease.

GARDEN BUGS OF THE SOUTH & SOUTHEAST

In everyday language, we commonly refer to insects, spiders, and other creepy-crawly organisms, such as centipedes, as bugs. They, or signs of their presence, are routinely encountered in gardens and yards. Within this diverse mix are a wide variety of "bad" bugs, regularly referred to as pests, and "good" bugs, which are often considered beneficial. Most garden pest species cause damage by directly feeding on plants, transmitting disease to plants in the process, or by indirectly damaging or disturbing plants by their activities. The resulting damage can be simply aesthetic or can lead to poor plant performance, deformed growth, reduced yield, or even death. Other pests can cause damage to structures or present a nuisance by their presence.

Beneficial species are a gardener's best friends. They provide natural pest control by feeding on or parasitizing undesirable garden and landscape bugs, helping to keep their populations in check. Others deliver key services such as decomposition, nutrient recycling, or pollination. Many are also entertaining or attractive and add to the overall enjoyment of the garden.

Controlling Pests

It's temping to want to reach for a container of pesticide at the first sign of a pest problem. This strategy, however, can often be counterproductive. Many commonly available pesticides can be harmful to humans, other wildlife, and the environment, especially if overused or applied inappropriately. Beneficial insects, such as monarchs and bees, are particularly susceptible. Harming these "good" bugs depletes your garden's natural pest control measures.

A better and more sustainable approach is to use integrated pest management, referred to as IPM. IPM focuses on long-term prevention, not just short-term control. Monitoring is the first step. This is best done by regularly getting out into your garden or landscape and looking around. Do you see any obvious signs of pest presence or plant problems? If you do, take a closer look and try to identify the culprit. Use this guide as an aid. You can then take a sample to a local extension agent or nursery professional for confirmation. Next, it's important to assess the scope of the problem. Is it limited to a particular branch or plant, or is it impacting a larger area or number of plants? No matter what, regular monitoring is always a great strategy, as it helps you identify pest issues before they become problems. Remember, most large pest outbreaks start out small.

Now that you have identified the pest and level of infestation, you can develop a plan to control it or decide that control is not required at this particular time. IPM employs a management approach that typically involves a combination of mechanical, biological, and chemical controls to specifically target the pest of concern.

Removing small numbers of Japanese beetles by hand is a mechanical control option.

Mechanical control can include physically removing pests from plants, using traps or barriers, or otherwise making a less suitable or desirable environment for the pest.

Biological control uses known natural enemies against the pest. This can be a predator, parasitoid, or even a pathogen. A classic example is using ladybugs to help control aphids.

Ladybugs are a popular biological control option.

Chemical control, especially broad-spectrum insecticides, should be a last resort.

Chemical control makes use of pesticides. Pesticides should only be used when necessary. Less-toxic alternatives such as horticultural oils or insecticidal soaps are often used first, and treatments are always applied only to the infected plant to minimize nontarget impacts. Remember, when using chemicals, always carefully follow the label directions for application rates and safety precautions.

Healthy & Diverse Landscapes

Healthy plants are more resistant to attack from pests and disease. Therefore, regular garden care and maintenance, along with a little TLC, is a great way to help prevent problems. Healthy plants also look and perform better, produce more flowers, and offer higher quality resources for pollinators.

Healthy plants, like this bee balm, will welcome beneficial insects and resist pests more effectively.

Landscapes with higher levels of plant diversity, particularly flowering plants, tend to attract and maintain a higher abundance and wider range of beneficial insects. Collectively, such basic methods are easy to implement and offer a strong first line of defense.

A wide variety of flowering plants invites more beneficial pollinators to your yard.

Good Plants for Beneficials

Beyond preying on pest species, many beneficial insects also feed on pollen and nectar. They are therefore attracted to landscapes with an ample supply of floral resources. While there is no shortage of wonderful blooming plants to choose from, there are some basic tried-and-true (and readily available) choices. These include many common bedding plants, wildflowers, and herbs.

Common herbs, such as this dill, attract many pollinators.

If allowed to flower, dill, fennel, borage, rosemary, thyme, mint, and basil are magnets for beneficial species.

Many daisy-like flowers (Asteraceae) such as zinnias, cosmos, Indian blanket, purple coneflower, coreopsis, goldenrod, and sunflowers are equally attractive.

Sunflowers and other profusely flowering plants make your yard an insect magnet.

Dutch White Clover, while nonnative, is a great option to make a bare spot on a lawn or a garden more attractive to wildlife.

Lastly, clovers, partridge pea, dotted horsemint, buck-wheat, and sweet alyssum are all fantastic. Whether planted alongside vegetables in the home garden, included more broadly in the larger landscape, or simply placed in a container or window box, they will not fail to provide color and attraction.

BUTTERFLIES & MOTHS
Order Lepidoptera

Silver-spotted Skipper
(Epargyreus clarus)

wingspan up to 2.4 inches; stout body; wings brown with a prominent white patch on the hindwing below; larvae feed on various pea family plants, including *Wisteria* spp. and false indigo bush (*Amorpha fruticosa*); larvae make leaf shelters

Long-tailed Skipper
(Urbanus proteus)

wingspan up to 2 inches; wings brown with blue-green iridescence above; hindwing with long tail; larvae make leaf shelters on host plant; feeds on various wild legumes; can be minor pest of garden peas and beans

Horace's Duskywing
(Erynnis horatius)

wingspan up to 2 inches; wings brown with small translucent spots on forewing; female has more contrasting darker brown markings and larger forewing spots; rests and feeds with wings open; avid flower visitor

Fiery Skipper
(Hylephila phyleus)

wingspan up to 1.5 inches; wings above dark brown with orange markings in males; females with reduced orange markings; wings below yellow-orange with scattered small dark spots; short antennae; avid flower visitor; low, erratic flight; larvae feed on various lawn grasses, including St. Augustine grass but are not considered a pest

Whirlabout
(Polites vibex)

wingspan up to 1.5 inches; wings above orange with dark brown borders in males; females dark brown with light spots; short antennae; avid flower visitor; low, erratic flight; larvae feed on various lawn grasses, including St. Augustine grass but not considered a pest

Brazilian Skipper
(Calpodes ethlius)

wingspan up to 2.45 inches; wings elongated; wings above dark brown with large translucent spots; hindwing below reddish-brown with translucent spots in the center; larvae feed on native and ornamental *Canna* species and can cause severe aesthetic damage; larvae make rolled leaf shelters

Polydamus Swallowtail
(Battus polydamas)

wingspan up to 4.5 inches; wings black with broad yellow spot band along the outer margin; lacks hindwing tail; continuously flutters wings while feeding; larvae feed on pipevine; primarily limited to Florida peninsula and southern Texas

Black Swallowtail
(Papilio polyxenes)

wingspan up to 4.25 inches; wings black with yellow spot band; female with reduced yellow bands and blue scaling on hindwing; hindwing with single tail; abdomen with yellow spots; larvae feed on carrot family plants, including dill, sweet fennel, and parsley

Black Swallowtail Larva
(Papilio polyxenes)

2 inches long; green with black bands containing yellow spots; feeds on carrot family plants, including dill, sweet fennel, and parsley and can be a minor garden pest

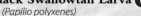

Eastern Tiger Swallowtail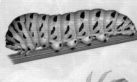
(Papilio glaucus)

wingspan up to 5.6 inches; wings yellow with bold black stripes in males; wings yellow or black in females; the females mimic toxic pipevine swallowtail; generally feeds with wings outstretched

Giant Swallowtail V
(Papilio cresphontes)

wingspan up to 5.8 inches; wings
above dark brown with crossing yellow
spot bands; wings below yellow;
hindwing with single tail; tail with
central yellow spot; avid flower visitor;
larvae feed on *Citrus* plants, including
cultivated citrus

Giant Swallowtail Larva V P
(Papilio cresphontes)

up to 2.3 inches long; mottled brown
with a cream saddle and rear end;
feeds on *Citrus* plants, including
cultivated lime, orange, and lemon;
can be a minor foliage pest

Cabbage White P
(Pieris rapae)

wingspan up to 2 inches; wings
white with black forewing tops and
black spots; non-native; larvae are
pests of various cabbage-family
vegetables, including cabbage,
broccoli, cauliflower, and kale

Cabbage White Larva P
(Pieris rapae)

up to 1.2 inches long; green to
blue-green with short hairs, a narrow
yellow stripe and yellow spots; feeds
on various cabbage-family vegetables,
including cabbage, broccoli, cauliflower,
and kale

Orange Sulphur V
(Colias eurytheme)

wingspan up to 2.3 inches; wings
orange with black borders in male;
yellow-orange in females; some females
white; hindwing below yellow with
central pink-rimmed silver spot; larvae
feed on clovers and alfalfa

Cloudless Sulphur
(Phoebis sennae)

wingspan up to 3.25 inches; wings mostly unmarked lemon yellow in males; lemon to pale yellow with narrow dark border and central spot on forewing in females; seasonally variable; avid flower visitor; feeds with wings closed; migratory

Cloudless Sulphur Larva
(Phoebis sennae)

up to 1.8 inches long; green to yellow with a bright yellow stripe and blue spots along the side and numerous small black spots; larvae are green if feeding on leaves, yellow if feeding on flowers; feed on various *Senna* spp.

Great Purple Hairstreak
(Atlides halesus)

wingspan up to 2 inches; wings above iridescent blue with black borders in males; dusty blue in females; wings below dull black; hindwing with two hair-like tails; abdomen orange-red; larvae feed on mistletoe

Red-banded Hairstreak
(Calycopis cecrops)

wingspan up to 1.2 inches; wings above brown with some light blue scaling; hindwing below gray-brown with broad red band edged in white; hindwing with hair-like tail

Gray Hairstreak
(Strymon melinus)

wingspan up to 1.4 inches; wings above dark gray with orange-capped black spot on hindwing; hindwing below light gray with white-outlined black line and orange-capped black spots near single hair-like tail; avid flower visitor

Cassius Blue
(Leptotes cassius)

wingspan up to 1.2 inches; wings above lavender blue in males; white and pale blue with dark borders in females; hindwing below gray-brown with white banding and orange-rimmed dark eyespot; larvae feed on *Plumbago*

Monarch
(Danaus plexippus)

wingspan up to 5 inches; wings orange with black veins and borders; avid flower visitor; migratory; larvae feed on milkweeds

Monarch Larva V
(Danaus plexippus)

up to 2 inches long; banded with yellow, white, and black; has two black filaments on each end; feeds on milkweeds; populations declining

Zebra Heliconian P
(Heliconius charithonia)

wingspan up to 4 inches; elongated black wings with yellow stripes; elongated body; long-lived; state butterfly of Florida; adults feed on nectar and pollen; roosts communally at night

Zebra Heliconian Larva V
(Heliconius charithonia)

up to 1.5 inches long; white with black spots; numerous black branched spines; gregarious when young; feeds on passionflower vines

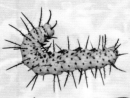

Gulf Fritillary V
(Agraulis vanillae)

wingspan up to 4 inches; elongated forewing; wings above orange with black markings; hindwing below brown with elongated silvery spots; migratory, avid flower visitor

Gulf Fritillary Larva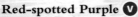
(Agraulis vanillae)

up to 2 inches long; orange with black branched spines; may have darker lines; feeds on passionflower vines

Mourning Cloak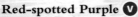
(Nymphalis antiopa)

wingspan up to 4 inches; wings above brownish-black with jagged margins, a broad yellow border and blue spots; wings below black with gray striations resembling bark; adults do not visit flowers but feed on tree sap and fermenting fruit; larvae feed on willows, elms, hackberries, and poplars

Red-spotted Purple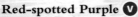
(Limenitis arthemis astyanax)

wingspan up to 4.3 inches; wings above black with blue iridescence; hindwing below black with blue iridescence and bold orange spots; adults seldom visit flowers; larvae feed on black cherry, deerberry, and willows

Red Admiral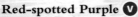
(Vanessa atalanta)

wingspan up to 3 inches; wings above black with reddish-orange bands; forewing with white apical spots; larvae feed on false nettle, pellitory, and nettles; particularly common in spring

Question Mark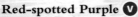
(Polygonia interrogationis)

wingspan up to 3.25 inches; wings above orange with black spots, irregular margins and a hooked forewing; hindwing with short tail; wings below mottled brown and bark-like; seasonally variable; hindwing above black in summer form, orange in winter form; adults feed on tree sap and fermenting fruit; larvae feed on elms, hackberries, nettles, and false nettle

Luna Moth  V
(Actias luna)

wingspan up to 4.25 inches; wings green with violet margins; hindwings with long tails; hairy white body; males with large ferny antennae; adults regularly come to artificial lights at night; larvae feed on hickories, walnuts, persimmon, and sweetgum

Cecropia Silkmoth V
(Hyalophora cecropia)

wingspan up to 5.75 inches; wings brown with pale margins, a red and white band, and a prominent central light crescent spot; hairy red and white body; males with large ferny antennae; adults often come to artificial lights at night

Cecropia Silkmoth Larva V
(Hyalophora cecropia)

up to 4.5 inches long; bluish-green body with bright blue, red, and yellow tubercles, each with short black spines; larvae feed on a wide range of different trees and shrubs

Polyphemus Moth V
(Antheraea polyphemus)

wingspan up to 5.8 inches; wings tan to warm brown; hindwing with large eye-spot; males with large ferny antennae; adults regularly come to artificial lights at night

Polyphemus Moth Larva V
(Antheraea polyphemus)

up to 3 inches long; bright green body with thin yellow vertical stripes and a brown head; larvae feed on various trees and shrubs

Royal Walnut Moth Larva  🅥
(Citheronia regalis)

up to 5.5 inches long; greenish-blue
body with orange head; long, curved
red and black horns; pupates in soil;
larvae often found wandering on the
ground; feed on walnuts, hickory,
sumacs, and persimmon

Rosy Maple Moth 🅥
(Dryocampa rubicunda)

wingspan up to 2 inches; bright pink
and yellow wings; fuzzy yellow body;
larvae feed on maples; adults come
to artificial lights at night

Hummingbird Clearwing 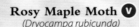 🅥
(Hemaris thysbe)

wingspan up to 2.2 inches; stout, hairy
body with olive thorax and reddish-
brown abdomen; wings reddish-brown
with clear patches; adults day flying; avid
flower visitor; feeds like a hummingbird

Tersa Sphinx Larva 🅥 🅟
(Xylophanes tersa)

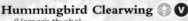

up to 3 inches long; green or mottled
brown with a pair of prominent eyespots
toward the head and a curved horn on
the rear; feeds on various plants, including Egyptian starcluster; minor foliage
pest; adults visit flowers for nectar

Carolina Sphinx Larva
Tomato Hornworm 🅟
(Manduca sexta)

up to 4 inches long; bright green body
with white diagonal stripes along sides
and a curved horn off the back; larvae
feed on tomatoes, potatoes, and bell
peppers; larvae can defoliate plants

Eastern Tent Caterpillar 🅟
(Malacosoma americanum)

length up to 2 inches; black with a
cream stripe on back, blue spots on
side, red-brown hairs; black head; defo-
liating pest of various landscape trees

Bagworm Moth (P)
Family Psychidae (several species in South)

up to 2 inches long; builds brown, cocoon-like structure with bits of leaves and twigs that conceal the larva inside; hangs from branches; larvae feed on various trees and shrubs; foliage pest when in large numbers

Cabbage Looper (P)
(Trichoplusia ni)

up to 1.5 inches long; light green with thin light stripe on the side; moves like an inchworm; pest of various vegetables and flowers, readily feeds on cabbage, kale, broccoli, cauliflower, and collards

Fall Webworm (P)
(Hyphantria cunea)

up to 1 inch long; greenish to brown body with long light hairs, broad mottled stripe, yellow spots and black bumps; head may be black or red; larvae feed together inside loose silken web on a wide variety of wild and ornamental trees; foliage pest that primarily causes aesthetic damage

Squash Vine Borer Moth (P)
(Melittia cucurbitae)

wingspan up to 1.5 inches; black thorax, antennae, and forewings; abdomen orange with black spots; adults are day flying and visit flowers; larvae are white with a black head and resemble grubs; bores into the stems of squash, pumpkins, gourds, cantaloupes and melons

Southern Armyworm (P)
(Spodoptera eridania)

up to 2 inches long; green to blackish body with a brown to reddish brown head; a broad pale side stripe, black spots, and other narrow pale stripes; larvae are gregarious when young; feeds on a wide range of vegetable and flower species and can cause significant feeding damage

May/June Beetle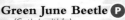
(*Phyllophaga* spp.)

up to 1 inch long; stout, unmarked shiny tan to reddish-brown oblong body; clumsy flying adults readily attracted to artificial lights on spring or early summer nights; larvae live underground

May/June Beetle Larva 🄿
(*Phyllophaga* spp.)

up to 1.7 inches long; white, C-shaped grubs with a dark head; live underground and feed on plant roots and decaying organic material; can damage lawns, vegetables, and flowers when in high numbers

Green June Beetle 🄿
(*Cotinis nitida*)

up to 1.2 inches long; robust, oblong green body with brownish-yellow side stripes and a varying degree of brownish-yellow on the wing cases and thorax; adults damage ripening fruit of various plants, including apples, peaches, pears, grapes, and berries; larvae feed on organic material in soil

Colorado Potato Beetle 🄿
(*Leptinotarsa* spp)

up to 0.4 inch long; oval, cream to tan body with black stripes and a slightly orange thorax (pronotum) marked with black; bulbous larvae are reddish marked with black spots; pest of various nightshade family plants, including potato, eggplant, and tomato

Grapevine Beetle 🅅 🄿
(*Pelidnota punctata*)

up to 1.2 inches long; oblong, yellow-brown to tawny orange with a few black spots along the side; feeds on grape leaves and fruit but only a minor pest; adults attracted to artificial lights at night

Lady Beetle (convergent)  **B**
(Hippodamia convergens)

up to 0.3 inch long; oblong body; bright orange wing cases spotted with black and a black thorax (pronotum) marked with two converging white dashes; highly beneficial predator of insect eggs and soft-bodied pests, including mites, aphids, thrips, and mealybugs

Lady Beetle Larva **B**
(Family Coccinellidae)

up to 0.25 inch long; elongated black body with orange spots; resembles a tiny alligator; highly beneficial predator of insect eggs and soft-bodied pests, including mites, aphids, thrips, and mealybugs

Polished Lady Beetle **B**
(Cycloneda munda)

up to 0.25 inch; oblong body; wing cases unmarked orange; thorax (pronotum) black with white markings; highly beneficial predator of insect eggs and soft-bodied pests, including mites, aphids, thrips, and mealybugs

Firefly **V**
(Family Lampyridae)

up to 0.8 inch long; flattened dark and elongated body with orange and yellow markings; underside tip of abdomen is pale and produces light; larvae are predators of insect larvae, snails, and slugs; common sight on spring and summer nights

Fiery Searcher **V** **B**
(Calosoma scrutator)

up to 1.30 inches long; robust body with iridescent green wing cases edged in copper or violet, a violet thorax (pronotum), and powerful jaws; quick and voracious predators of insect larvae, including many pest species

Japanese Beetle  **P**
(Popillia japonica)

up to 0.5 inch long; metallic green
with copper-colored wing coverings
and white tufts along the abdomen;
nonnative; adults feed on the leaves
and fruit of many landscape and garden
plants, including roses, apples, maples,
blueberries, elms, corn, and zinnias;
grubs are pests of turf and can cause
serious damage to lawns

Spotted Cucumber Beetle **P** **D**
(Diabrotica undecimpunctata)

up to 0.25 inch long; wing cases are
yellow with black spots; adults feed on
leaves, flowers, and fruit; larvae attack
the roots and stems; vectors of plant
disease; feeds primarily on squash,
melons, and cucumber

Little Leaf Notcher **P**
(Artipus floridanus, FL only)

up to 0.55 inch long; oval dull white to
light bluish body with noticeable small
pits and a slightly elongated snout;
adults feed on the leaves of various
fruit, vegetable, and ornamental plants,
including citrus, azalea, collards, and
hibiscus; larvae feed on plant roots

Red-headed Flea Beetle **P**
(Systena frontalis)

up to 0.20 inch; oval metallic black body
with a reddish head; adults jump when
disturbed; adults feed on leaves and
fruit of various nursery, berry, and vegetable species; larvae feed on plant roots

Vegetable Leafminer P
(Liriomyza sativae)

up to 0.10 inch long; tiny; yellow and black body with transparent wings; larvae feed within leaf tissues, causing visible pale trails; feeds on wide variety of vegetables, including beans, tomatoes, melons, and peppers

Crane Fly V
(Family Tipulidae)

up to 2.5 inches long, including legs; slender body with very long, thin legs and two elongated wings; resembles a large mosquito; larvae feed on organic matter; adults are harmless and do not bite

Mosquito Larva P
(Family Culicidae)

up to 0.20 inch long; aquatic living near surface; elongated brown segmented body with no legs and a long breathing siphon on the rear end; often wiggles back and forth in the water

Lovebug P
(Plecia nearctica)

up to 0.35 inch long; elongated dull black body, black wing, a red thorax, and long legs; often seen when they're mating; occasional large outbreaks; nuisance pest around home; can mark car paint and windshields

Long-legged Fly V B
(Family Dolichopodidae)

up to 0.35 inch; metallic green to copper body; bright eyes; mostly transparent wings and long, thin legs; often seen perching on leaves; adults prey on pests, including aphids, spider mites, thrips, and whiteflies

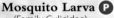

Robber Fly
(Family Asilidae)

up to 1 inch long; highly variable in appearance; typically slender body with a tapered abdomen; large eyes; two wings; and long, bristly legs; opportunistic predators of other insects; perches on vegetation or structures and flies out to capture prey

Florida Bee Killer
(Mallophora bomboides)

up to 1 inch long; black and yellow hairy body with a tapered abdomen; large eyes; two black wings and long, bristly black legs; resembles a bumble-bee; opportunistic predator of bees and wasps; perches on vegetation or structures and flies out to capture prey

Greater Bee Fly
(Bombylius major)

up to 0.50 inch long; bulbous body with generally golden-brown hair; two clear wings edged with black, and a rigid, forward-pointing proboscis; resembles a small bumblebee; adults hover and feed at flowers; larvae are parasites of bee and wasp nests

Flower Fly
(Sphaerophoria spp.)

up to 0.40 inch long; dark head and thorax; elongated yellow and black or brown-striped abdomen, two transparent wings; adults feed at flowers; larvae are predatory on aphids

House Fly
(Musca domestica)

up to 0.30 inch long; gray hairy body with black stripes on the thorax, two transparent wings, and red eyes; attracted to garbage, animal waste, and decaying material

Asian Tiger Mosquito 🅿 🅳
(Aedes albopictus)

up to 0.40 inch long; black body and legs marked with white; females bite to collect a blood meal; considerable nuisance and occasional disease vector

Southern House Mosquito ⊛ 🅿 🅳
(Culex quinquefasciatus)

up to 0.17 inch long; narrow, striped body with two wings, long, thin legs and a prominent proboscis; females bite to collect a blood meal; considerable nuisance and occasional disease vector

Tarnished Plant Bug 🅟 🅓
(Lygus lineolaris)

up to 0.25 inch long; oval body marked with yellow, brown, and black; long antennae; feeds by piercing plant tissues; attacks a wide range of vegetable, fruit, and landscape plants; transmits plant diseases

Leaf-footed Bug 🅟
(Leptoglossus phyllopus)

up to 0.80 inch long; brown, elongated body with a pale band across the center, long antennae, and flattened projections on the hind legs that resemble leaves; pest of many plants, including vegetables, fruits, berries, nuts, and ornamentals, especially when numerous

Cicada Nymph Exoskeleton 🅥
(Family Cicadidae)

up to 1 inch long; non-living translucent stout brown papery molted skin with an opening down the back; typically found on tree trunks, vegetation, or even on the sides of buildings

Candy-striped Leafhopper 🅥 🅟 🅓
(Graphocephala coccinea)

up to 0.35 inches long; elongated body, red with blue stripes, and yellow legs and undersides; adults hop and fly; feeds on plant juices from leaves and stems; minor pest of berry plants, native and ornamental trees; can transmit plant disease

Oleander Aphid 🅟 🅓
(Aphis nerii)

up to 0.10 inch long; bulbous yellow body with black legs, antennae, and eyes; has two black pipe-like projections on the abdomen; adults may or may not have wings; nymphs look like small adults; feeds on plant sap and is a pest of oleander and milkweeds; produces honeydew that also causes sooty mold on plants

Green Peach Aphid 🅿 🅓
(Myzus persicae)

up to 0.08 inch; tiny, bulbous yellow-green body with dark eyes; adults may be winged or unwinged; feeds on plant juices; pest of peaches, plums, and apricots, vegetables, flowers and ornamental plants; produces honeydew that can lead to sooty mold on plants

Silverleaf Whitefly 🅿
(Bemisia tabaci)

up to 0.04 inch; tiny, yellow body with dark eyes and four white wings held over the back like a tent; nymphs have an oval flattened body and are wingless; feeds on plant sap; pest of wide variety of vegetable and ornamental plants; secretions can lead to sooty mold on plants

Wheel Bug 🅑
(Arilus cristatus)

up to 1.25 inches long; body gray to dark brown with long legs and antennae; prominent rounded spiked crest on the thorax; narrow head with long beak for capturing prey; adults and nymphs are predators of insects, including many pest species; typically found on vegetation

Large Milkweed Bug 🅥 🅿
(Oncopeltus fasciatus)

up to 0.70 inch long; elongated oval red and black body; feeds on plant sap from leaves, stems, and seeds of milkweed and oleander; adults may also consume aphids and monarch eggs and young larvae; northern populations migrate to the south to overwinter

Spined Soldier Bug 🅑
(Podisus maculiventris)

up to 0.60 inch long; mottled brown shield-shaped body with one spine on each shoulder and a dark diamond on back where the wings overlap; predatory, feeding on insects, including many common pests

Green Stink Bug ⓟ
(Chinavia hilaris)

up to 0.75 inch long; green shield-shaped body with slightly darker diamond shape on the back where wings overlap; nymphs wingless and marked with black, orange, yellow, and white; feeds on plant juices; pest of many vegetable, fruit, and landscape plants

Harlequin Bug ⓟ
(Murgantia histrionica)

up to 0.40 inch long; red and black marked shield-shaped body with a black diamond on back where the wings overlap; feeds on plant juices; attacks many vegetables and fruit trees

Southern Chinch Bug ⓟ
(Blissus insularis)

up to 0.25 inch; elongated oval body with either long or short white wings marked with black; major pest of St. Augustine grass, a common lawn grass

Mealybugs ⓟ
(Pseudococcus longispinus, various)

up to 0.15 inch long; oval body with waxy white secretions often producing a spiky or cotton-like appearance; males have wings; feed on plant juices; cause leaf discoloration, distorted growth, and disease transmission; produce sugary secretions that promote sooty mold

Asian Citrus Psyllid ⓟ
(Diaphorina citri)

up to 0.15 inch long; elongated mottled brown body and wings; wings held over the back like a tent; nymphs have yellow-orange oval bodies with white, waxy secretions produced off the rear; transmits the disease that causes citrus greening

TRUE BUGS
Order Hemiptera

Azalea Lace Bug  ⓟ
(Stephanitis pyrioides)

tiny, up to 0.06 inch long; adults have cream colored bodies with long antennae, lacy-looking wings, and a hood over the head; nymphs are black and cream with spiny projections; pest of ornamental evergreen azalea varieties; feeds on leaves, causing a bleached or stippled appearance

Soft Scale Insects ⓟ
(Suborder Sternorrhyncha)

up to 0.12 inch long; typically oval with a somewhat flattened body; produce white cottony secretions; feed on plant juices; pests of various landscape plants, fruit trees, and ornamental plants; produce sugary secretions that promote sooty mold

THRIPS
Order Thysanoptera

Thrips ⓟ
(Order Thysanoptera)

up to 0.08 inch; tiny elongated yellow-green bodies with pale, feathery wings; feeds on plant juices; cause plant discoloration or deformation; attack many plants, including vegetables, fruit trees, berries, flowers,l and ornamentals

Green Lacewing
(Chrysoperla spp.)

up to 0.70 inch long; light green slender
body, long antennae, golden eyes,
and four transparent wings with
green veins; adults feed on pollen
and nectar; often attracted to artificial
lights at night

Green Lacewing Larva B
(Chrysoperla spp.)

up to 0.50 inch long; elongated mottled
brown body tapered toward the rear;
large jaws; resembles a small alligator;
ferocious predator of soft-bodied pests,
including aphids, whiteflies, spider
mites, and thrips

Leafcutting Bee
(Megachile spp.)*

up to 0.80 inch long; most have a stout, black body with a compact, striped abdomen; many hold wings out to the side when foraging; collects pollen on the underside of its abdomen (often resulting in a yellow belly); cuts circular pieces of leaves for nest construction; resulting holes are best sign of its presence

European Paper Wasp ⊕ Ⓟ Ⓑ
(Polistes dominula)

up to 0.50 inch long; elongated black body marked with yellow; four narrow amber wings; a distinct waist between the abdomen and thorax; social; invasive; often constructs nest on structures; adults are predatory on other insects, including pest species; can sting

Fine-backed Red Paper Wasp ⊕ Ⓟ Ⓑ
(Polistes carolina)

up to 1.2 inches long; elongated rust-colored body, four narrow black wings; and a distinct waist between the abdomen and thorax; colonial; often constructs nest on structures; adults are predatory on other insects, including pest species; can sting

Common Thread-waisted Wasp ⊕ Ⓑ
(Ammophila procera)

up to 1 inch long; black head and thorax, long thin legs, four narrow dark wings, and an orange and black abdomen with a long, narrow waist; nests in the ground; adults are predatory on other insects, particularly larvae

Black and Yellow Mud Dauber ⊕ Ⓟ
(Sceliphron caementarium)

up to 1 inch long; black body marked with yellow; long thin legs, four narrow dark wings, abdomen with a long, narrow waist; preys on spiders; build nests out of mud, often on structures

Green Metallic Sweat Bee
(Agapostemon spp.)

up to 0.50 inch long; head and thorax metallic green, dark narrow wings; abdomen metallic green or yellow with black bands; avid flower visitor

Common Eastern Bumblebee
(Bombus impatiens)

up to 0.90 inch long; fuzzy, robust body with a black-and-yellow pattern, four black wings; carries pollen on its hind legs; colonial, nests in underground cavities

Eastern Carpenter Bee
(Xylocopa virginica)

up to 0.9 inch long; robust; head, wings, and abdomen black; thorax with yellow hair; beneficial pollinator; constructs nest in wood and can cause structural or aesthetic damage to buildings; primarily attacks unpainted or untreated wood

Western Honey Bee
(Apis mellifera)

up to 0.75 inch long; fuzzy appearance, black eyes, four amber wings; black-and golden-orange-striped abdomen; carries pollen on back legs; produces large colonies; can aggressively defend hives; exceptional pollinator

Double-banded Scoliid Wasp
(Scolia bicincta)

up to 1 inch long; black body; four black wings with metallic blue sheen; abdomen with two cream bands; larvae are parasitoids of beetle grubs

Eastern Yellow Jacket
(Vespula maculifrons)

up to 0.70 inch long; black-and-yellow body; four dark wings; yellow-striped abdomen; constructs papery nests, adults prey on other insects, defends nests and stings; seeks out sugary foods

Southern Yellow Jacket
(*Vespula squamosa*)

up to 0.70 inch long; elongated black and yellow body; four dark wings; yellow striped abdomen (often more yellow than eastern yellow jacket); colonial; constructs papery nests often in cavities; adults are predatory on other insects, including pest species; aggressively defends nests and stings; seeks out sugary foods and can be a nuisance

Red Imported Fire Ant
(*Solenopsis invicta*)

up to 0.25 inch long; reddish-brown body with black rear end; produces large colonies; builds conspicuous mounded ground nests; stings aggressively; omnivore; invasive

Slender Twig Ant
(*Pseudomyrmex gracilis*)

up to 0.40 inch long; slender, brown to orange-brown body, with an elongated slender waist; produces small nests in vegetation; omnivore; painful sting; invasive

Odorous House Ants
(*Tapinoma sessile*)

up to 0.12 inch long; tiny, dark brown to black body; can form large colonies; seek out sugary foods, considered a nuisance pest

Carolina Mantis V B
(Stagmomantis carolina)

up to 2.6 inches long; long, slender green-to-brown body; triangular head; enlarged front legs for grasping prey; immatures lack wings; adults have four wings; found on vegetation; camouflaged; occasionally attracted to artificial lights at night; predatory, feeding on other insects

Northern Walking Stick V
(Diapheromera femorata)

up to 3.70 inches long; elongated narrow greenish-brown-to-brown body; very long thin legs, long antennae; highly camouflaged, resembles a twig; lacks wings; feeds on shrubs and tree leaves

Two-striped Walking Stick V
(Anisomorpha buprestoides)

up to 2.60 inches long; elongated dark brown body with black stripes; long legs and antennae; resembles a dead twig; often seen when mating; males much smaller than females; feeds on leaves of various trees and shrubs; sprays a defensive secretion if disturbed

MANTISES

STICK INSECTS

EARWIGS
Order Dermaptera

Ring-legged Earwig P B
(Euborellia annulipes)

up to 0.65 inch long; elongated dark
brown body; wingless; prominent
pincers on the end of the abdomen;
dark band around each leg; often
found under objects; omnivorous,
occasionally nibbles on plants;
beneficial predator of other insects

GRASSHOPPERS, CRICKETS, & KATYDIDS
Order Orthoptera

Field Cricket V B
(Gryllus spp.)

up to 1.2 inches long; dark brown
to black with membranous wings,
enlarged hind legs, long antennae,
and two prominent tail filaments;
omnivore; produces loud chirping calls

Southern Mole Cricket P
(Neoscapteriscus borellii)

up to 1.70 inches long; brown, elongated
body with membranous wings; long
hind legs; stubby front legs for digging;
long antennae; two prominent tail
filaments; pest of turf and lawns

Greater Angle-winged Katydid V
(Microcentrum rhombifolium)

up to 2.40 inches long; green body with
long hind legs; membranous green
wings; long antennae; resembles a leaf,
highly camouflaged; feeds on vegetation; produces loud rhythmic calls at
night; often attracted to artificial lights

Eastern Lubber Grasshopper V P
(Romalea microptera)

up to 3 inches long; yellow-to-orange-
brown body marked with black to an
all-black body marked with yellow or
red; large hind legs, long antennae;
short membranous wings; feeds on
foliage of various plants

American Cockroach Ⓥ Ⓟ
(Periplaneta americana)

up to 2 inches long; oblong, reddish-brown body, spiny legs, and long antennae; adults have brown membranous wings; common under objects or mulch; scavenger; nocturnal

Subterranean Termite Ⓟ
(Reticulitermes spp.)

up to 0.60 inch long; whitish to amber body with a somewhat darker head; reproducing adults have dark bodies and four transparent wings; colonial; resembles winged ant; decomposer; structural pest

COCKROACHES & TERMITES

DRAGONFLIES & DAMSELFLIES

Eastern Pondhawk Ⓥ Ⓑ
(Erythemis simplicicollis)

up to 2 inches long; males have a powdery blue body; females have a green body and white-and-black spotted abdomen; both with four unmarked transparent wings; immatures are aquatic; adults are active aerial predators

Common Whitetail Ⓥ Ⓑ
(Plathemis lydia)

up to 2 inches long; male with stout chalky blue-white abdomen and wide central black band on wings; female with pale spotted brown abdomen and two black wing bands

Eastern Amberwing Ⓥ Ⓑ
(Perithemis tenera)

up to 1 inch long; small; male with amber-orange wings; female with clear wings marked with brown patches; abdomen striped with brown and yellow

Two-spotted Spider Mite (P)
(Tetranychus urticae)

up to 0.03 inch long; oval yellow to orange body; four pairs of legs; often two visible dark side spots; resembles a tiny spider; feeds on plant sap and spins loose silk on vegetation; pest of many trees and shrubs, vegetables, and berries

Sowbug and Pillbug (B)
(Order Isopoda)

up to 0.45 inch long; dark gray to brown, oval body, with plate-like segments and seven pairs of small legs; feeds on decaying plant material; found under objects, leaf litter, and mulch

Millipede (B)
(Order Julida)

up to 4.5 inches or more; typically dark-colored; smooth, cylindrical worm-like body with many small legs; often curls up when disturbed; found under objects, leaf litter, or mulch; feeds on organic material; harmless

Earthworm (B)
(Superorder Megadrilacea)

up to 8 inches or more; elongated, smooth, segmented, cylindrical reddish-brown to gray body; found in soil; somewhat slimy; feeds on organic material

Garden Snail (B)
(Cornu aspersum)

highly variable size, 0.20 to 4 inches; brown to dull-colored fleshy body with elongated stalk-like tentacles off the head; a hard shell on the back; feeds on organic material

Milky Slug (P) (B)
(Deroceras reticulatum)

up to 2.30 inches long; elongated mottled gray to brown slimy body with a hump on the back; two stalk-like tentacles off the head; pest of vegetables, flowers, and some fruits

Harvestmen/Daddy Longlegs Ⓥ Ⓑ
(Order Opiliones)

up to 0.30 inch long with much longer legs; small, round, brownish body with eight thin, long legs; scavenger or predator, feeding on other insects and invertebrates

Centipede Ⓑ
(Class Chilopoda)

up to 5 inches; typically tan, dark brown, or gray segmented and flattened wormlike body with many legs that extend outward; predator of insects and other invertebrates; can bite

Yellow Garden Spider Ⓥ Ⓑ
(*Argiope aurantia*)

up to 2.5 inches long; abdomen egg-shaped with black and yellow markings; eight black legs marked with yellow or red; females much larger than males; spins large, circular web with distinctive central zigzag pattern to capture prey

Golden Silk Spider Ⓥ Ⓑ
Banana Spider
(*Trichonephila clavipes*)

up to 1.50 inches long; tan elongated abdomen with yellow spots; silver body; eight long black, orange, and yellow legs; female much larger than male; spins large circular webs between vegetation or on structures

Carolina Wolf Spider Ⓑ
(*Hogna carolinensis*)

up to 2 inches long; hairy gray to dark brown body with darker markings; eight long legs; resembles a small tarantula; predatory, feeds on other insects and invertebrates; nocturnal; occasionally wanders into homes